MW01289640

THE
MURDER
OF
MICHAEL
JACKSON

THE COVER UP &
CONSPIRACY

Deborah Stefaniak

ISBN-13: 978-1505842845
ISBN-10: 1505842840

Any "Homicide" investigation warrants the question, "What was the motive?".

In the case of Dr. Conrad Murray there was none. He would have made more money keeping Michael Jackson alive.

For some others, however, there were many.

CONTENTS

cov·er–up a planned effort to hide a dishonest, immoral, or illegal act or situation.

con-spir-a-cy Criminal conspiracy is an agreement between two or more persons to commit a crime at a point in the future. Criminal law in some countries may require that at least one overt act must also have been undertaken in furtherance of that agreement, to constitute the offense. There is no limit on the number participating in the conspiracy and, in most countries, no requirement that any steps have been taken to put the plan into effect For the purposes of concurrence, the act is a continuous one and parties may join the plot later and incur joint liability. Conspiracy can be charged where the co-conspirators have been acquitted or cannot be traced.

MARCH, 2011

It was mere days after the passing of Elizabeth Taylor. She was a dear friend of Michael Jackson's and someone I had known to stand by his side in his time of need. Both she and Michael were gone now. I sat at my computer in the kitchen thinking how nice it would have been to have met her and thank her for her friendship and support of a man I had come to know in such an extremely unorthodox way.

Michael Jackson and I had somehow been connected throughout his life. I'd receive "visions", I'd call them. He'd be sitting on a plane or watching TV. Sometimes we'd even "talk", although not out loud. The talks turned into conversations and the conversations often turned into meetings.

He had passed over however. And with his passing I thought the "visions", the talks, and the connection would follow. They didn't. They continued.

Continuing the journey from my original book, **Another Part of Me; An Extraordinary Tale of Twin Souls**, I will describe the events that have transpired since the death of Michael Joseph Jackson in relation to his murder. These events and visions I have received, have allowed me to see the real person that killed Michael Jackson. Sorting through the evidence, I was astounded to see that all of it was there from the very beginning of the trial of Conrad Murray.

As you follow this story along, you may recall the findings and evidence presented in that trail, the evidence presented in the Katherine Jackson vs AEG trial, and the ongoing dispute between the Michael Jackson Estate and Michael's previous manager, Tohme Tohme.

The circumstances and people in Michael's life will be presented in such a way, that you too will finally know the truth about what really lead to the murder of one of the most famous entertainers and humanitarians in the history of our planet – Michael Jackson.

WORDS FROM BEYOND

In the instant I thought of her, she was there. Striking violet eyes I had never seen, but had always been told about. Raven hair and a warm welcoming smile. "Thank you so much for all you did for Michael", I said. She laughed. The kind of laugh that would come from deep inside the pit of your stomach; Contagious, completely, and utterly heartfelt.

We spoke for moments it seemed, reminiscing on how it would have been nice to meet in the physical. How I one day had wanted to meet her and offer my thanks for being such a great friend to Michael. Elizabeth Taylor was surprising. Not only to have been "visiting" me, but her sheer presence, her laughter and her humility, seemed to be a complete package I had never expected.

I smiled and was delighted at her visit. When I had thought she had left I could hear her voice. "Michael. You have to tell her why you're here." I froze. I had seen Michael. He had appeared as a full apparition in front of my television set a few days after he passed. He was present in my meditations and I had seen his life pass before my eyes, even feeling the expanded state of his energy joining with the all. I thought I had sent him on. I didn't want to keep him here. He deserved to be happy.

When I asked him what happened he told me very little; "Someone gave me a shot and everything went black. I didn't kill myself." I had thought perhaps there was an accident. Maybe he just wanted me to know it wasn't his fault. Yet here he was, still in my home and I didn't even know it.

My mind searched for reasons why he might still be with me. Did he need something? Was something left unfinished? Did he need to say something directly to me that he hadn't said? Our time, I thought had passed. We had missed the opportunity to come together physically, so why was he still hanging around?

At the moment I posed the question in my mind, the answer came. He was there to help me. Somehow help me traverse through life. After his physical death, my life too had come to an end. It wasn't physical. It was emotional, mental and spiritual.

I was left alone and apparently he wanted to help. I was reluctant. He should move on, not be forced to stay with me for any reason. He deserved to be happy. Yet at the moment, I didn't realize what that meant.

Several months had passed. I still questioned why Michael would be with me. He seemed to stay back from me, observing. Then just when I didn't expect it, I'd hear his voice. A sarcastic and funny comment or a pleading not to yell at my dog. It was delightful in a way. I had begun to know him on a day to day basis of how he really was in life, not just in our conversations that seemed to be from afar. He was funny, sensitive and would often call out to "Elizabeth!" for help when he was at his wits end with my pity parties.

He had proven to be trustworthy and a good friend. He told me about the real motives behind peoples intentions and although I never wanted to believe him, he was always right. I marveled at his wanting to be with me. So when we began to talk about his death, I began to get the feeling that there was more at play than I had once thought.

As anyone might ask a friend, one day I just came out with it. "So what happened anyway?" He had told me just after his death that someone had given him a shot; everything went black; but that he didn't kill himself. Foolishly I thought it just meant he didn't overdose. Foolishly, I didn't even "think" about foul play.

It was when Elizabeth herself chimed in and said "The things they did to him were horrible. Just horrible" when I began to get that frozen, deer in the headlights feeling again. I was afraid. Something awful had happened and if I knew what it was, I wasn't sure if I was prepared to accept it.

I waited a few weeks to settle myself. If something had transpired, I'd need to be calm for him to tell me. We made an appointment. A set aside time when I could listen to all he had to say.

I took my notepad and sat on the couch. Michael had told me when he was living that he thought someone was trying to kill him. I passed it off. Maybe it was a psychotic fan or someone from his past. But this felt different and I knew I'd have to take notes.

Sessions like this I rarely would remember. I had spoken to the "other side" for others and often times the information would come fast and I never wanted to "judge" what came through. When that happens, you're just a medium, a conduit for information. Sometimes not even retaining what you said. With Michael, I needed the notes. If there was some sort of horrible circumstance that surrounded his death, I'd need to look into it. Get verification, then see if I could help.

The trial was just beginning for Conrad Murray that year. I quickly started a blog to document as much as I could. If he was truly murdered, if there was foul play at hand, I wanted people to know. I wrote down everything he said, but I doubted what he told me many times. Now as I look back after finding out the truth, his words shutter me, knowing what he said has been documented and in evidence with the LAPD since the investigation started.

"I was prepared to do the tour. I was giving it my all. They hired Murray to be my personal physician for the tour. They said they were afraid I couldn't handle it (Randy Phillips). When I went to the house I was met with a slew of them. Everyone from Phillips, DiLeo to Kenny Ortega. Conrad Murray told them he'd take care of me, except he didn't. Pretty soon I feel like I'm out of it.

He'd given me Propofol to sleep the night before. I was worried because I had these feelings about being murdered. I didn't know who, but I could feel it. It gave me chills. I was cold and my fingers were going numb. I used to say to Paris, Daddy's going to feel better one day. Then it became daddy needs to rest, to lay down and get well. She was like a little mother. She told me don't worry daddy. I'll take care of you.

The night I died I was staying upstairs. Everything that was said before about being murdered is right. There was no gun, no knife, no strangulation. Only a wish for me to go away. Sony wanted the rights to my catalog. It was all over the day I signed the contract. From that day forward everything changed. The Propofol was increased, and they took control of my life.

Randy Phillips and Kenny Ortega were my go to men. So I told them how I was feeling and Kenny became concerned. We worked together before.

Before I knew it, I felt drugged out of my mind. Murray walked out of the room and into the hall. The next thing I knew they entered the room again. He gave me a shot and said this will put you to sleep, but it didn't. I was still awake.

I didn't know what else to do. Everyone was running around trying to figure out what had happened. I was just standing there, not knowing what to do.

He was smoldering me with his spit in my mouth. I couldn't stand the sight of myself. I tried to talk but they couldn't hear me. Paris screamed "Daddy, daddy" and that's when everything went black again. Next I knew I was standing in your living room, bewildered. I didn't realize what had happened right away. It took me a while. No one could hear me. I knew I could reach you. I waited until it was time. Waited until I could talk and sit down so you could write. I'm not here to startle you. I'm here to help. To find peace and love. I love you more than you know.

A man put a needle in my arm – an IV drip in my leg. My arm was sore from pins and needles in my shoulder. I couldn't see. A brown haired guy. They were going through my papers. I could hear them. They ransacked the house. There was a security camera. It was pointed at the gate, but that night something wasn't right. My life was turning upside down and I didn't know why. I was out of my body, but not dead. He gave me the last shot and I died instantly. The man with the brown hair, short sleeved shirt, wide open collar, white. I hoped he'd come back to see more, but he didn't. He stayed away while Conrad Murray cleaned up. I just stood there watching, helpless.

He wrote down the time (Conrad Murray). It was significant. He had a pad of paper with him, taking notes. He said he carried it with him where ever he went. Black with leather trim. Frank was separate from this guy. They drove in separate vehicles. Sony = Mattola. Set AEG up to claim rights in return they would get profits from my Estate. Look for a contract between AEG and Sony. Executors of the will, Branca and McClain. They have a stake in Sony. They wanted control...out of money from the tour concerts This is It."

I was stunned at his words. Could it be true? It seemed so conniving, so amazingly brutal.

I began to watch the trial of Conrad Murray and tried to absorb as much as I could. If it was Conrad Murray that killed him, Michael would have said. But he didn't. He said "someone". And as far as I knew, he himself wasn't aware of who that "someone" was. He said he couldn't see.

GETTING IT OUT

As soon as I had begun the blog, Michael and I agreed I'd write what he needed me to. Get it out there. Those moments came sooner than I thought. There was a tribute concert scheduled with his family. A tribute concert that involved his children. He had me write several posts. He wasn't happy and there was a vast difference in his tone and feeling when he spoke. It wasn't just that the children would be involved and used in his place, it was because they didn't know "where the money was going."

Several months later I found out why. Articles surfaced that people from the show were not getting paid. The company that promoted the concert had filed for bankruptcy. There was more going on behind the scenes and Michael was watching. His children had remained in his heart and in his field of vision.

We made lists and statements about what we expected to come out. Michael wasn't eating, he didn't have an appetite. It seemed somehow he was being given things repeatedly that would make him weak. We noted blood, the syringe that would have killed him by the shot he described to me and the mention of other people. The first list was on 9/27/2011, the day of opening statements:

1. Closet evidence
2. Blood
3. Missing documents from his office
4. Time of death

5. Rubber gloves
6. The names of other people
7. Needle marks
8. Other drug administrations
9. Eating and diet/reduced appetite
10. Condition of his body when paramedics arrived
11. Paris/Prince testimony

On the second day of testimony we had already begun to see some of the evidence come forward. We, again, noted it in the post:

1. The concert tour was never intended just for 10 days. *(This was covered in my previous book Another Part of Me – An Extraordinary Tale of Twin Souls)*

2. Defense claims they can prove "scientifically" that Michael died instantly (This point was relevant because Michael also said he died instantly—someone had given him a shot)

3. The syringe - A syringe was found by the bedside with Propofol evidence in it. *(As stated previously, Michael had stated someone gave him a shot. This would be the evidence suggesting that.)*

4. Other people - Prior to opening arguments I stated "other" people would be brought up. Kenny brought up the email he emailed to Paul and Randy of AEG at 2 am in the morning *(Kenny must have been VERY concerned to email that late)* stating the concern of Michaels health.

5. The closet- brought up as the area where Murray stashed the drugs

6. His death was over money.

7. Kenny testified, as I stated earlier (previous blog posts) and in the same language (platform), that Michael wanted to use the performances as a "Platform" for sending a message to heal the world.

8. Other drugs - it was confirmed by testimony that there were other drugs found in Michaels system that contributed to his death that were administered by Dr. Murray

9. Timeline - earlier brought up and of course has been in the news. I expect more evidence as to the time of death to come. **During Michael's death I had birds pecking at my window (noted in previous book). My surmise was that he died well before paramedics were ever called.*

10. Defense stated the "perfect storm" was created by the drugs in Michael's body. Knowing he had a prior history of drug problems, what a better way to make it look like he killed himself. This was more like the "perfect murder" If he died immediately, why wasn't it reported immediately? I shuttered to know that Michael made it a point to say "I didn't kill myself."

11. Why would Murray record Michael apparently on drugs?

12. LaToya Jackson tweeted that she hoped someone would come forward with who else was in the house – She confirmed what Michael had stated previously, there was someone else in the home that night.

As testimony continued so did our posts. We went from Michael's words thanking his fans for their support and his wish for them to heal the world to further confirmations.

On 10/7/2011 we made another list:

1. Closet evidence. Turned out to be the place where bags where stored with Propofol

2. Blood : A bloodied shirt was found in his closet

3. Missing documents from his office I didn't see the whole thing-but there was a briefcase open in

the bathroom on the tub photographed.

4. Time of death. Evidence concludes his death was prior to paramedic arrival
5. Rubber gloves - Box of rubber gloves found in the closet
6. The names of other people - AEG executives, other doctors have been brought up
7. Needle marks -I'm sorry to say there were 13 puncture wounds shown on the autopsy report
8. Other drug administrations - Evidenced in his system were other drugs believed to contribute to his death.
9. Eating and diet/reduced appetite Michaels personal chef stated he wasn't eating.
10. Condition of his body when paramedics arrived – Michael was already gone when they arrived; eyes open and dry
11. Paris/Prince testimony - The family does not want these two to testify; however it's been stated they will if necessary

Murray certainly made it look like he did everything he could to save him. "I gave him CPR, I gave him mouth to mouth, I told someone to call 911, I told the ER doctors to try, try, try." The only thing wrong was that he knew by the time he did ANYTHING he already knew it was too late.

Conrad Murray stated he found Michael not breathing at 12:00. 911 wasn't called until 12:22 and that call was made by a security guard.

It was October, 2011 and ABC News reported that they had found additional fingerprints. Fingerprints that didn't match those of Conrad Murray. I was beginning to become hopeful. Waiting to see the truth of who really murdered Michael would come to the fore front. It didn't. The trial proceeded and Conrad Murray was found guilty of manslaughter and sentenced to an overcrowded prison.

Reports surfaced of Michael killing himself, that he was an addict. I could tell he was upset, when he began to make sure I told people he wasn't a "junkie".

On 11/11/2011 he had me write the following post:

"Due to the overwhelming feeling that Dr. Conrad Murray is not only guilty of my murder, but held accountable for my death, I felt it necessary to correct some statements in the general public.

My death was not brought about because of the negligence of one doctor. My death was brought about by the greed and manipulation of a contracting company who wished to retain the rights to my music catalogs. My life was incredibly insane. Full of people who wished to use my celebrity and status as a way to benefit themselves. Although I admit I had a problem with drug addiction, I did not, and I repeat, did not take my own life or contribute to it. I in no way shape or form took anything to deceive Dr. Murray or anyone else. My children and my heart are broken hearing these allegations that are false. No one would wish to step in my shoes if they knew what I had to go through. If I was an animal I might have been given better care. I was a person, a human being with feelings and a life. They took it from me, from my children, from you and it was all because of money.

Let me say this, no one and I mean no one on this planet can understand another person's life unless they have lived it. Leave me in peace."

Although the words were there, I still didn't get it. Why would a contracting company intent on concert performances be eager to get Michael out of the way?

ASKING THE QUESTIONS

I continued to follow the evidence as it came up. Conrad Murray decided to air a special that month. I watched intently as he boasted about who he thought Michael Jackson was and what good friends they were. He remarked about how dirty his home had been and repeated the fact, as he did during the trial, that he told Randy Phillips at AEG that he would make sure Michael would be at rehearsal - what does this say to you? I'll tell you what it said to me. It said Michael is something or someone "I" have control of. It says "Don't worry Randy, I'll take care of it for you".

In other words, he seemed to say I have control of the situation for you Randy. Nowhere did I hear any concern for "his friend" Michael. If Michael was the one that wanted him to be there as his doctor, why wouldn't his loyalties lie with Michael instead of Randy Phillips? I found out why later. AEG, the company Randy Phillips worked for, was the agency actually contracting the doctor and they were also the ones that were to pay him.

They also played the testimony of the girl Conrad Murray met during the airing. The one he was talking to on the phone that was brought up during the Conrad Murray trial. She said all of the sudden it seemed like Conrad had the phone in his pocket. She heard mumbled voices. It was stated that only Conrad Murray and Michael were in Michael's room the night he died during testimony. If Conrad and Michael were the only ones allowed upstairs and there that day and Michael was under or dead, who was Conrad Murray talking to? "I heard coughing and mumbling" she said. Who were these people? It was more evidence of others being there the night Michael was murdered.

One of the people Michael told me about, Frank DiLeo, had passed on in August that year. I looked for information on him. Any hint of testimony, or what he had to say about that night. I found a video of an interview he did. In it he explained that a fan called him while having an early lunch. It was 11:30, he said. Lunch had just arrived and she called to tell him an ambulance was at Michael's home. The ambulance didn't arrive until 12:20. It must have taken a long time to get lunch, I thought. He said he phoned Michael Amir, a security guard who was not yet present at the home, but delivered the message that "That's what he heard."

He also stated in that video that he was never paid by AEG. Yet in the emails discovered in the AEG vs Katherine Jackson trial, payments were being made for services from 6/29/09 on. He let us know that an attorney named Katz was brought in by Michael. Katz was also on the board for Sony. Later, because Katz was representing both AEG and Michael, Randy Phillips of AEG thought it best to bring in another attorney, John Branca, also on the board for Sony and present just prior to Michael's death.

DiLeo also stated that Paul Gongaware of AEG got cameras at the "last minute".

Apparently when Conrad Murray phoned Amir he testified that he said nothing about Michael's health. Yet both Frank DiLeo and Randy Phillips of AEG, during testimony in the Conrad Murray trial, had concluded that Michael was "having trouble breathing." That was some key information for not being present and no one to tell them what was actually going on. Not to mention that Randy's time of being informed of Michael "having trouble breathing" was said to be at 10:30 am. Hours before paramedics arrived. He had to be corrected by the prosecuting attorney, David Walgren.

Randy Phillips was the President and CEO of AEG; the "contracting" company for the This is It shows. In late August, 2008 a meeting was organized when Tom Barrack, head of Colony Capital, who owned the note on Neverland, contacted Phil Anschutz of AEG. They met at Colony Capital in Century City, Los Angeles and had a conversation about Michael doing some concerts.

Another meeting was set up at the Bel Air Hotel, with Dr Tohme, Michael's manager at that time and the man who negotiated the deal to save Neverland from foreclosure with Colony Capital. Tohme said that Michael wanted to tour with new music. This meeting was followed up with more phone conversations, meetings and negotiations.

Randy Phillips apparently came face to face with Michael and Dr Tohme in September, 2008 at the Bel Air Hotel. He said they had discussed the concept of the concerts and began to lay out a plan for Michael to tour. Phillips said that money was never discussed with Michael. He was only interested in the creative side of the plans.

At a meeting in Michael's home on October 31, 2008 Michael spoke about his reasons for touring again. He wanted to settle down with a good home for his family. Phillips said he felt they were living like "vagabonds." He said he was very emotional and both Michael and Randy Phillips ended up in tears.

This little part confirmed for me the statements Michael

had once made to me. He wanted a home, however, he didn't like to tour. However, a residence in Las Vegas would allow him to work and still stay in one place. Signing the contract for the "This is It" engagement just happened to include the home in Vegas and would allow him to have the opportunity to have a "normal" family home. For a man that had spent his entire life in the public eye, this one simple thing was extremely important to him.

Contracts were prepared and signed in January, 2009. Phillips stated during testimony, they stipulated thirty-one concerts.

Once the tickets went on sale, Phillips said they realized thirty-one shows were not going to be enough. They called Tohme Tohme, Michael's then manager, to ask Michael to do more shows and he said Michael agreed.

Phillips said he had no concerns about Michael's health that May during his testimony at Conrad Murray's trial, but heard in the first week of June that he was not eating and was losing weight.

This confirmed another item on our "list". Michael was not eating. Apparently, Murray attended a meeting and said that he was preparing protein shakes and a nutritional diet for Michael. When Phillips was asked about Michael's general health, he said that he was in good health. He was fine.

In early June, Michael began missing rehearsals and did not seem to be focused. As the production was due to move to London, Phillips said it was imperative that rehearsals were attended and performed well. Kenny Ortega's main concern was Michael's focus which was ordinarily extremely high and when Phillips tried to contact Michael by phone, he was not allowed to speak to him and was told he "was resting".

That must have been the "resting" part that Michael was referring to when he told me what he said to Paris. There was more information coming out and I was trying my best to see the real picture.

On June 20th Phillips had an email from Kenny Ortega and they arranged a meeting at Michael's house with Frank Dileo, Michael and Murray. It was insisted that Michael needed to focus as rehearsals were crucial at that time. They found out that Michael had been rehearsing at home with Travis Payne and as they left he told them; "You build the house, I'll put on the door and paint it!" Kenny Ortega replied "Great! That's all I wanted to know."

Michael was present at rehearsals on June 23rd and 24th and everything was back on track, Phillips testified. Yet this was the meeting Michael had told me about. Something was amiss. My feeling from Michael was that the meeting didn't go as well as Phillips testified it did. I later found out by testimony of his son, Prince, at the AEG trial, that during that meeting a vase was broken and there was a lot of yelling.

Other emails surfaced from Randy Phillips stating "this guy is really starting to concern me", in reference to Kenny and his concern for Michael's health. Phillips emailed Kenny that he should not play doctor or an amateur psychiatrist. His doctor, he said, was in control of the situation.

Further evidence came from the AEG vs Katherine Jackson trial, when an email was discovered from Michael's make-up artist dated June 22, 2009 that said Michael couldn't even walk down the ramp of the set without assistance and she referenced multiple letters from fans concerned about Michael's health and his severe loss of weight.

On June 25th, Phillips stated that Frank Dileo called Randy Phillips to tell him Michael had been taken ill. He drove quickly to the house in time to see the ambulance and the family cars leaving the property. He followed them to the UCLA Medical Center and was there all day.

Mr Chernoff, the attorney for Conrad Murray, began his cross examination of Randy Phillips at the Conrad Murray trial, with questions about the cancellation of the concerts. When asked about Michael's demeanor that June. Phillips replied "Genius! There is no entertainer in the world like him in the world today. His attention to detail was phenomenal!" Phillips said that at no time did he think Michael would not be able to complete the tour.

Later, during the Katherine Jackson vs AEG trial, emails were discovered between Randy Phillips and Colony Capital. They referred to a "broker" named Tohme Tohme who had somehow become Michael's manager after brokering the deal with Colony Capital to save Michael's ranch, Neverland. In those emails, Randy Phillips of AEG also stated to Richard Nanula of Colony Capital, that if Michael did not regain his confidence, the future looked "bleak". The deal was being set. Colony was to bail Michael out to keep Neverland, and in return Michael would have to perform under a contracting company named AEG. Even though, as Randy Phillips stated in his email, the future looked "bleak".

Additionally, emails surfaced referencing payments to Frank DiLeo from AEG. Payments that went past the date of Michael's death and that were categorized as "additional motion picture expenses". Those payments even brought questions from the AEG controller, Julie Hollander, like why the payments were continuing and that she was waiting for the Estate of Michael Jackson to "cry foul".

Others asked if the lump sum payment of $50,000 was made yet. It seemed evident Frank DiLeo was brought back into Michael's life by AEG, not Michael Jackson. Michael had fired him years prior and the payments to Frank on record seemed to only prove his alliances were not with his "client", but the company who had been paying him.

Frank resurfaced just prior to Michael's death, as did John Branca, the current executor of the Michael Jackson Estate and negotiator for the "This is It" film released on October 28, 2009, just four months after Michael's passing.

I needed to find more information so I looked at Conrad Murray's statement he made to the LAPD on June 27, 2009 and noted the following:

"It was 4:30 in the morning and he was wide awake. And then he complained, I got to sleep Dr Conrad. I have these rehearsals to perform. I must be ready for the show in England. And tomorrow I will have to cancel my performance. I have to cancel my trip."

"I wouldn't want to sign the death certificate when I don't understand the cause of his death. And therefore I recommended we have an autopsy."

"His show was going to fall apart. He needed to sleep."

In reference to the lawyers, Jermaine Jackson and AEG asked him to review the press release. Conrad states: "I added that the cause - although it was presumed to be a possible cardiac arrest, the underlying cause of that condition is not known until an autopsy is performed."

"I had two syringes - and they were. I would recap them. . . .Everything that I use I would put it quickly into the bags."

His statement to the police confirmed other details. Michael stated to me that he was still wide awake, when Conrad Murray came in and told him "it would put him to sleep." It also raised a question: if Murray was actually guilty of giving him too much Propofol, why would he ask for an autopsy?

Another man testified at the Conrad Murray trial; Alberto Alvarez, the security guard to first come upon the scene with Dr. Murray and Michael in his bedroom. At the Conrad Murray trial Alvarez testified how Murray immediately instructed him to help gather up empty medicine vials and put them in a plastic garbage bag. Murray also told him to remove one of two drip bags from an IV stand next to the bed—the one that contained a bottle with a milky-looking medication inside.

In my opinion, a guilty doctor would be very careful to make sure all the evidence was cleaned up. Yet when the investigator on the scene, Elissa Fleak testified the following statements were made:

"There was a syringe on the table and one on the ground, next to the bed.

Fleak: Yes.

Fleak: It was on the ground near the bottle on the ground.

Q: Did you ask for these things to be fingerprinted?

Fleak: I don't remember?

Q: Is it part of your role to ask for things to be fingerprinted?

Fleak: No.

DDA showed photos of the syringes, an oxygen tank, other items, taking Investigator Fleak through identifying photos with more items, including an IV bag with connected tubing during her testimony.

Fleak: Yes. And in the tubing hand an IV in it?

Halfway from the tubing there was a clamp and that clamp had a syringe in it. The plunger was depressed."

I also found that at the end of the interview by LAPD, Dr. Murray was asked for the keys to his car.

It was reported that inside the BMW they found a contract between AEG Live and Murray saying he would be paid $150,000 a month to work as Jackson's doctor, along with AEG Live President Randy Phillips business card and cell phone number. Later, during the AEG trial with Katherine Jackson there was also an email presented that stated Randy Phillips and Dr Murray were responsible for MJ rehearsals and attendance schedules.

During Mr Walgren's cross examination it was established that while the Defense's testing was being performed, Dr Shafer had asked the company for the information and the methodology used. The company did not respond to him. Miss Brazil, Assistant District Attorney, had also asked for that information and the company had referred her to Flanagan. When she threatened to invoke the Court, she was then given a copy. The witness did not know why the Prosecution copy had notations on it that were not present on the Defense copy.

They were quick and precise in the findings of manslaughter for Conrad Murray. The trial itself was a few months, ending with his sentencing on November 7, 2011.

It seemed the prosecution had a plan and was keen on implementing it. Defense counsel was silenced whenever they tried to bring up additional evidence. Interviews outside the courthouse that day included Conrad Murray supporters that said the real murderer of Michael Jackson was somewhere out dining in Beverly Hills and that somebody was hiding in the house. Some wanted Conrad Murray to file for a motion for a new trial immediately and to appeal at a later time on the grounds that information about a third party presence was not used.

A fingerprint on the syringe bag, a slashed syringe bag, and missing bottle of Propofol and a missing surveillance tape all indicated that somebody else was in the house and got out with the surveillance tape. They claimed that was the murderer and that Dr. Murray did not kill his friend.

When asked if they were actually saying there was a conspiracy, the answer was yes.

Some statements made during the trial of Conrad Murray could have provided the key information his supporters were looking for.

Conrad Murray's defense attorney Chernoff stated:

MJ was ultimately responsible for the production costs up until June 22, 2009?

Phillips: Yes

Chernoff: Contractually he was responsible for tens of millions ... (objection sustained)

Chernoff: AEG had cancellation insurance. (objection sustained)

Insurance. This was big red flag, although I didn't realize it at the time.

A few months after the death of Frank DiLeo, Michael paid me a visit; WITH Frank DiLeo. Frank apologized to me for his part in Michael's death, although at the time I had no idea what he was speaking about.

It was on 11/13/11. He said:

There was a contract between him and Live. (Referring to AEG Live)

There was an intent to commit fraud with the insurance company.

The security was paid by Live (referring again to the contracting company, AEG Live)

Someone was to be paid off by the Estate through Live

I started to do some digging. It didn't gel with me. How could I know there was more, find the evidence later myself when the LAPD couldn't?

My feelings turned from couldn't to wouldn't, when more information was discovered.

I found that the District Attorney at that time was Steven Cooley. He was the one that took center stage when Conrad Murray was found guilty. Matter of fact, prosecuting counsel David Walgren received a promotion soon after Murray was convicted. It looked nice on the surface, but what the public didn't know is that Steven Cooley had a reputation for receiving "contributions". It's been reported that he apparently never held a "murder" trial and on his list of major contributors I found AEG Live, the contracting company involved with Michael Jackson at the time of his death.

TIMOTHY LEIWEKE LOS ANGELES, CA PRES/CEO/AEG WORLDWIDE, INC. $1500 Contribution date: 2010-10-28

Further investigation turned up an "Amici Curiae" requested by Mr. Cooley on behalf of AEG Live. That document was filed with the State of California, County of Los Angeles on August 31, 2011. It prevented certain information to be revealed to Lloyds of London, the insurance company suing AEG Live, to be put into evidence until the conclusion of the Conrad Murray trial.

The document stated that the criminal case for Dr. Murray would be impacted if this information were to be disclosed. In my opinion, it most certainly would. Had that evidence been brought out in court, Dr. Conrad Murray may have never been convicted.

Another former prosecuting attorney, Richard I Fine, PhD., stated publically that there was a preposterous amount of judicial briberies in the system. Most of them taking money from trust accounts to pay judicial officials off.

Some people have surmised that this too may have been the reason that the 2002 will that Michael himself asked to be returned to him from his former lawyer, John Branca in 2003, was allowed to be entered with the courts.

Branca and McClain, the executors of the Estate of Michael Jackson, are both shareholders in Sony/ATV. John Branca was also a subject of investigation for conspiracy and embezzlement during Michael's 2005 child molestation charge and a close friend of Tommy Mottola.

In 2011 it was reported that the Estate used the "trusts" set up by the Michael Jackson estate to purchase EMI Publishing. It seemed the Estate was diverting funds in salaries, other trusts, and purchases of assets in collaboration with Sony/ATV, the company Michael so vocally spoke against back in 2001 and the company who's catalogs he held half ownership in.

Distribution rights for the "This Is It" film were also sold to Sony Pictures, another unit of Sony Corp., for $60 million. A claim that AEG executive, Randy Phillips stated publically that he was involved in. The movie went on to gross $252 million worldwide, the most of any concert film ever.

It was reported that the men administering Michael Jackson's estate were seeking 10 percent of profits they were able to generate from the late pop superstar's work. Attorney John Branca and music executive John McClain filed a motion in 2010 asking the court to approve the compensation. They were seeking to run a company that would oversee a business based on the work of Michael Jackson. That request was asked to be expedited that March.

Then on March 15, 2010, nine months after Michael Jackson's death, the news surfaced that his estate had signed one of the biggest recording contracts in history. It gave Sony the rights to sell his back catalog and draw on a large vault of unheard recordings. The deal, for recordings through 2017, guaranteed the Jackson estate up to $250 million in advances and other payments. It also offered an especially high royalty rate for sales word wide.

VISIONS

I continued to keep an ear and eye out for more information. I kept asking Michael who it was that actually killed him, but I was met with silence. We continued to write together and he started to bring me more people to meet from the "other side". I met his ex-sister in law, Dee Dee, a grandfather of his named Prince and then the visions that I had received while he lived began to continue. Only this time they were visions of him on the "other side".

The first was very simple. He was just standing there, outside a castle, speaking with Princess Diana. I had heard they were friends when they both lived. I knew he admired her. Later he told me that they had become good friends. They both had to leave children behind, he said, and they found a lot in common.

Elizabeth Taylor continued to visit with Michael often and before I knew it, other people who had passed also had something to say about Michael's death. Elizabeth explained that a person named Tohme Tohme was named in an insurance policy and Diana came herself one night to let me know there were more people involved in Michael's murder than I had thought. Who, was the question. I felt like I was being given bits of information, yet nothing was coming together. I needed to find out who actually killed him so I could work backwards to gather the evidence.

In the next few years more evidence came, but still no killer. Katherine Jackson filed suit with the "contracting" company Michael spoke about. AEG Live was brought to trial on the implication that they hired and controlled Dr. Conrad Murray. The trial was not televised, as requested by the counsel for AEG. I'd soon find out why. It was during that trial that the most horrific evidence yet was presented.

Pictures of a gaunt Michael appeared. His health was failing and his body was described as "skeletal" by crew working on the "This is It" concert series. I could see his pale face and even see the fear in his eyes in several photos. When he told me he was afraid someone was trying to kill him, it was a complete understatement. He was terrified.

Terrified was not an understatement either. Emails during the AEG trial surfaced and it was the emails from Randy Phillips of AEG himself that spoke the loudest:

"He's an emotionally paralyzed mess, filled with self-loathing and doubt now that it is show time. He is scared to death. Right now I just want to get through this press conference."

"I just slapped him and screamed at him louder that I did with Arthur Cassell"

"I screamed at him so loud the walls are shaking"

"Tohme and I have dressed him and they are finishing his hair. Then we are rushing to the O2. This is the scariest thing I have ever seen."

Kenny Ortega's email on 6/19/2009 stated he was "feeding him and wrapping him in blankets."

Yet even with all the emails Phillips continued to add concert dates.

Although the trial itself was not publicized, some of the information did make its way out. There were comments from Michael Jackson's stylist and later from the production manager that he was pretty thin in his last two weeks. One of them, production manager Bugzee Houghdahl, wrote, "He needs some cheeseburgers with a bunch of Wisconsin cheesehead bowlers and a couple of brats and cheese. Jeez." That was just 11 days before Michael died, but four days later, Bugzee had a more serious assessment of Jackson's condition, writing, "I've watched him deteriorate in front of my eyes over the last eight weeks. He was able to do multiple 360 spends back if April. He'd fall on his ass if he tried now."

Soon the news reported the most devastating witness's testimony of all. Karen Faye, Michael's make-up artist said that costume director Michael Bush looked in horror at Michael's unclothed body before a dress rehearsal. He said "Oh my God. I could see Michael's heart beat through the skin of his chest."

It was that same music director who revealed on June 16, 2009 that Michael was not able to sing live and dance. Michael had been putting down "tracks" to use during the show because of it.

Kenny Ortega, the man Michael explained to me that was his "go to" man, had emailed Randy Phillips to make sure he knew what was going on. Ortega said "He's terribly frightened it's all going to go away. He was like a lost boy." But Phillips shot down Ortega, and warned him not to "play" doctor. He refused to consider stopping the concerts. He said "You cannot imagine the harm and ramifications of stopping the show now."

Depositions from AEG executives revealed that they insisted Michael was healthy enough to do "100 shows" in the days before the rehearsals. The emails found in the AEG vs Jackson case confirmed they had full knowledge of the health concerns presented. At that time, it would have been difficult for Michael to perform ten, let alone 100 shows.

Mere days after the emails surfaced, on September 10, 2012, the news came that AEG was dropping their insurance claim with Lloyd's of London, the underwriter who was suing AEG for not disclosing the state of Michael's health.

Lloyd's of London wanted AEG to have a doctor give Michael a complete medical examination before it would expand its policy to include illness. The company wanted five years of medical records, including information about Michael's fitness program. Lloyd's stated their requests were always met with "no response."

Time was running short at that time. With dates close to performance time and a policy that went into effect on June 22, 2009, but still required additional disclosures that couldn't be met, I'm sure there had to be quite a bit of pressure on AEG. Numerous articles surfaced with Randy Phillips being quoted as saying they had millions of dollars at stake.

AEG asked Conrad Murray, to gather the information for the cancellation insurance, which concerned Michael's health. On June 25, Murray replied to the company at 11:17 am that authorization was denied. The emails he sent to Lloyds were presented at the Conrad Murray trial. According to the times, Michael was dead less than an hour after they were sent. Paramedics received their first call to the residence for a 50 year old male, not breathing at 12:22. When they arrived his eyes were open and dry, mouth open. Paramedics on the scene testified that the time of death was most likely at least one hour before the call was made.

Conrad Murray must have been busy that morning. TMZ reported that the same day, the day of Michael's death the owners of a storage facility in Texas said two women filled out a contract on April 1, 2009. They rented a unit in the name of Dr. Conrad Murray's medical practice. Dr. Murray's credit card was used to pay the rent for the unit. The unit contained boxes, furniture and other items. The two women arrived at 9:22 AM - 3 hours before the 911 call from Michael's home.

According to Murray's cell phone records in the Murray trial, five text messages were sent to or from Texas during the hours of 8:29 am and 12:04 pm the day Michael died.

They weren't the only ones looking into storage facilities. That same day Michael's personal assistant, Michael Amir said he wasn't at the home earlier because he was googling storage facilities as well. He was in the shower, he said, when Conrad Murray phoned him for help.

Michael Amir stated he was going in later that day, just in time to take Michael to rehearsals. Yet when I looked back at Kenny Ortega's testimony, he stated that Randy Phillips was going to pick Michael up on June 25, the day of his death. "They were meeting for some reason then he was going to bring him to rehearsals."

Amir also testified he didn't speak to anyone but two of the security guards that day. When Mr. Chernoff cross examined him during the Conrad Murray trial, showing phone records with a call with Frank DiLeo, he then remembered getting the call on the way to the home.

Ortega said he called Phillips that day to say how excited he was to go to rehearsals that afternoon. He said that Phillips told him when he called, that he was at the house. "There was an ambulance leaving the property."

In the aftermath, after Michael was pronounced dead, Michael Amir returned to the property on Carolwood where Michael was staying. He took part in a police interview and was then met by a NEW security team hired by Tohme Tohme. Michael Amir and his team were then released. With no one any longer at the home, one could only fathom what this NEW security team was for. After all, Tohme was on record as being released from his contract from Michael months earlier. Although it is still unclear where a $100,000 a month contract he held with AEG stood at that time.

When Michael stated to me early on "There was a security camera. It was pointed at the gate, but that night something wasn't right." it began to make sense. LaToya Jackson, Michael's sister, stated publically that she requested to view the security footage from the night before and day Michael passed. That request was denied, she said. Apparently, the footage in question was erased. In several public interviews she stated that they were already in the house and they didn't want anyone to see who was leaving.

I also noted in Amir's testimony that he phoned another security guard before speaking with Alberto Alverez, the first security guard apparently to come on the scene. Even though the security house was closer to the kitchen door, Alverez was instructed to use the front door. Sometimes, he said, that door was unlocked.

39

What the interesting note here is, however, is that he phoned that same security guard the night Michael was arriving home from rehearsals. He said it was to "make sure everything was in order for their arrival." Yet he didn't recall phoning him on the day of Michael's murder.

I wondered "who" exactly Michael Amir Williams was taking orders from. It was discovered in the AEG vs Katherine Jackson trial that it was AEG who was paying him directly, as well as another security guard named Alberto Alvarez.

Further investigation into the home itself revealed two staircases leading to the upstairs where Michael was. One was at the front door, where Alverez was instructed to go by Michael Amir, and the other was by the kitchen door, the door closest to the security house.

It was peculiar, especially when the AEG vs Katherine Jackson trial came into view. Emails surfaced from fans showing concern for Michael. Michael was apparently reaching out to them, letting them know how stressed and worried he was about being able to perform 50 shows. They even witnessed bones protruding from his shoulders and down his back. These were the same fans that after 15 years of following Michael closely were now suddenly denied access to him. Michael Amir, Alberto Alverez and Faheem, all security guards for Michael, had begun to restrict access to him and they weren't even allowed to give a letter to him without "security" reading it first they said.

Alvarez, Muhammad and Williams ended up all being represented by the same attorney, Carl Douglas, during the investigation into Michael's death.

Other emails, like the one from Kenny Ortega on June 20, 2009 asked where his assistant (Michael Amir Williams) was that night and stated he was massaging his feet to calm him and calling his doctor. No one was caring for him, he said, and there were four security guards outside his door and not one of them even offered him a cup of tea to warm him from the chills he was having.

Faheem Muhammed even testified in the Conrad Murray case that he had to actually "go get" the nanny. Where was she when the children were upstairs crying for their father?

Apparently, according to his testimony, the nanny was with the children when Alvarez was first instructed to enter the home. The problem I had with all these testimony's is that they didn't add up. Alvarez made several statements to police. The first statement did not mention cleaning up any bottles or vials at Murray's direction, but the second did. Further he drew a photo of a saline bag at Murray's trial. The photo he drew did not depict a bottle inside of it, but the prosecuting attorney, David Walgren, carried a saline bag up to him with a Propofol bottle in it for confirmation that it was that exact scene he was describing.

Later ABC News reported that fingerprints were tested on all the items Alvarez stated he touched in the "clean up" being done at the request of Dr. Murray. None of the items had his fingerprints on them.

The insurance policy was in force as of June 22, 2009 for $17.5 million. Effective just three days prior to Michael's passing. Insurance that AEG had filed to collect on within a week of Michael Jacksons death on June 25, 2009.

It was during the AEG trial that the "contract" also came out. It was true. The contract with AEG and Michael outlined a specific plan. Michael would get the house he so desperately wanted, but with a price. He would perform all the concert dates that AEG and his manager at the time, Tohme Tohme would set for him.

Ten shows went to fifty, even though it was evident from the very beginning that AEG executive Randy Phillips was doubtful that Michael would regain his confidence to perform them.

Even at the announcement of the shows, Randy Phillips emails relayed that Michael was in no condition to perform. Yet they added shows after the announcement, twice, collecting millions of dollars in ticket sales. Phillips refused to stop the "This is It" concerts, saying "You cannot imagine the harm and ramifications of stopping the show now".

That March Phillips was even quoted in the press as saying Michael called him all the time and that on a Wednesday afternoon (March 11) he told him "Randy, Randy, no more shows, no more shows".

In an email dated February 27, 2009 Paul Gongaware of AEG stated AEG was holding all the risk. At this time ten shows were on track, but Paul continued that if Michael did not approve of more they would go WITHOUT his approval.

It wasn't something Michael agreed to. As the contract stated, those discussions and agreements were between AEG and Tohme Tohme, Michael's manager. Not only were the number of shows agreed upon by them, but the payments as well. All payments would go to Tohme, through Michael's own company Tohme was controlling.

The contract added an additional $100,000 per month, payable directly to Tohme himself from AEG, Michael's "contracting" company.

If Michael didn't perform all the concerts as they agreed, he would lose his "catalogs" and all assets that belonged to him, as per the contract. The prized Beatles catalog and the items he told me about repeatedly in the days prior to the Conrad Murray trial.

The exhibits in the Jackson vs AEG trial allowed me to view it in black and white. I was in shock. The mere words on the contract itself were written in a way that Michael himself would receive nothing. His manager at the time, Tohme Tohme, would be in control of the money, if any was ever given, while Michael himself had everything he owned at stake.

As the evidence rolled out, further incrimination surfaced of Michael's "contracting" company. Emails surfaced from Randy Phillips again stating Michael's death was "a terrible tragedy . . but life must go on." He additionally stated "AEG will make a fortune from merch sales, ticket retention, the touring exhibition and the film/dvd" Phillips wrote in fact AEG Live would be allowed to sell Jackson tour merchandise and share in the profits from the documentary "This is It', produced from rehearsal video.

Yet as I recalled the "rehearsal video" he was apparently referring to, was only supposed to be Michael's own personal video. As testified in the Conrad Murray trial.

Kenny Ortega said:

"We didn't film for that documentary. Michael was filming for his personal use".

When Chernoff, the attorney for Conrad Murray asked if there was "other" footage taken from April through July, Ortega said: "There weren't always cameras rolling. They were always IF he asked"

It was stated there were only two cameras; both for Michael's personal footage. Later, when the video for "This is It" was released, there were 37 camera credits on the sleeve.

An email from Paul Gongaware of AEG was revealed that was sent to Randy Phillips, which noted taking out the shots of MJ in the red leather jacket at the soundstage where the mini-movies were being filmed. He looked way too thin and skeletal, it said.

It was Sony's attorney, Gary Bostwick who stated during the Conrad Murray trial that: "There were more than two cameras". He also said he was reluctant to hand over the footage during the trial. He said they would hate for anything to go viral.

I later found that Randy Phillips from AEG himself stated that there were over "100" hours of footage taken during the rehearsals.

THE DOCUMENTS

On July 2, 2009, just one week after Michael's death Associated Press reported "AEG chief: Jackson rehearsal footage may become motion pic" "May" was an interesting word to me. Considering the fact that it was AEG themselves that filed for copyright to the footage days after Michael's death, specifically stating the words "Motion Picture". The "recorded" copyright was on the same date: July 2, 2009.

Type of Work: Preregistration
Type of Work Preregistered: Motion Picture
Preregistration Number / Date: PRE000002493   /
2009-07-02
Application Title: Documentary footage re rehearsals and behind the scenes for Michael Jackson ?This Is It? Concert Tour
Title: Documentary footage re rehearsals and behind the scenes for Michael Jackson ?This Is It? Concert Tour
Copyright Claimant:AEG   Live,   LLC.   Address: 5750 Wilshire Blvd., Suite 501, Los Angeles, CA, 90036.
Creation of Work Began: 2009-04-13
Date of Anticipated Completion: 2009-09 (Approximate)
Projected Date of Publication:2009- (Approximate)
Authorship on Application: AEG Live, LLC.
Description of Work: Audiovisual recordings shot in the Los Angeles, California area by and on behalf of documentarians Tim Patterson and Sandrine Orabona (as work for hire) in connection with preparations and

rehearsals for Michael Jackson?s ?This Is It? Concert Tour. Includes footage shot at (1) Center Staging in Burbank, California from May 18, 2009 through June 1, 2009, (2) Stimulated, Inc. in Burbank, California on May 29, 2009, (3) Culver Studios in Culver City, California on June 1, 2009 through June 10, 2009, (4) the Forum in Inglewood, California on June 1, 2009 through June 21, 2009, and (5) Staples Center in Los Angeles, California from June 22, 2009 through June 25, 2009. Footage includes, inter alia: (1) On-stage rehearsals, creative meetings, and behind-the-scenes footage of Michael Jackson and/or band, dancers, and singers. With Michael Bearden (musical director), Alfred Dunbar (bass), Roger Bashiri Johnson (percussion), Jonathan Moffett (drums), Thomas Organ (guitar), Orianthi Panagaris (lead guitar), and Morris Pleasure (keyboard); singers Judith Hill, Dorian Holley, Darryl Phinnesse and Kenneth Stacey; director Kenny Ortega; choreographers Travis Payne, Anthony Testa, and Stacey Walker; Karen Faye Heinze (hair and make up); Michael Bush (costumes); other members of the crew and other persons (including personnel of Stimulated, Inc.); and fans; and (2) Michael Jackson singing and dancing in 3D and 2D formats, for the background Chaos LED screen to be set onstage behind him during his performance. Also footage shot by Steve Stone Productions at the Nokia Theater in Los Angeles, California and Center Staging in Burbank, California from April 13, 2009 through May 2009 of dancers? auditions for Nicholas Bass, Daniel Celebre, Mekia Cox, Christopher Grant, Misha Hamilton, Shannon Holtzapffel, Devin Jamieson, Charles Klapow, Ricardo Reid, Danielle Rueda Watts, Tyne Stecklein, and Timor Steffens.

Names: AEG Live, LLC

I say "recorded" because it had to have been submitted prior to 7/02 to be recorded with the office. Michael died on a Thursday, 6/25. This "motion picture" had to be sent by mail. Considering the time for the US postal service to deliver, when do you think this was prepared and mailed? Most likely over the weekend when Randy Phillips and Tohme Tohme, who had been let go by Michael in May, met with John Branca and John McClain, the executors for Michael's estate. All of this done within ONE WEEK of Michael's passing.

It was that day, June 28, 2009, when Randy Phillips and Tohme Tohme signed a contract agreeing to budgeted amounts for production costs and pool expenses they were to be reimbursed for from the Estate. Tohme signed on behalf of the Michael Jackson Co, LLC.

Yet on January 14, 2009, there was an email brought forth in the AEG vs Katherine Jackson trial. It clearly stipulated that Michael Jackson was the sole officer and only one able to sign on behalf of the entity. This was beyond the fact that Michael himself issued statements that he had fired Tohme.

Additional emails that came to the forefront included this one, with Randy Phillips now boasting about footage that was earlier stated, never taken:

"We just closed a $60m deal against a gigantic back-end for the rights to the film that will be created from all the footage we so wisely shot from the beginning of this project to the last rehearsal."

That "deal" was with the Estate of Michael Jackson, John Branca and John McClain, who also happen to sit on the board for Sony Corporation, not to mention another intruder that came back into Michael's life just prior to his death; Frank DiLeo.

Sony may seem irrelevant for some, but it was Michael himself that held protests against Sony at the time he had released his last studio album entitled "Invincible" in New York City, USA. He said he was going to be a free agent. That Sony was mad and that he owned ½ of Sony/ATV at that time. His contract with them only required him to give them "a few songs". Ones that he had already written. It was the catalogs he so often spoke about that were included in his ½ of Sony.

It was reported in 2012 that Sony itself announced in December, 2008 cuts of 16,000 workers after the global financial crisis hit, but it had not managed to make a profit since.

CLARIFYING VISIONS

It seemed there was ample evidence that many things had gone wrong, but still nothing to tell me who actually killed him. Nothing until the first of July, 2013.

At the time I had been receiving visions of Michael on the other side. Inside, however, there were indications that something else was happening. I could hear him at times coming it seemed from within me. It was a soul thing, I thought. Somehow since I was able to see him, perhaps we were joining in some fashion more so since he had passed. There is a school of thought that the I AM presence or higher self of us all join at some point in time. Maybe it was that the allowed me to see what I did. All I know is that it took me by surprise, and at the time, confused me even further.

I was awakening in the morning hours. It was usually that time when contact with Michael was the strongest. It was the time before waking consciousness and the subconscious mind. That time is special, because it is the time when you can most remember the intuition of the soul. Whether it be through dreams or feelings, they often play out and if we can remember them, we can get a glimpse of the actual knowings known to the universe itself.

This time it was different, however. Most times it would be Michael. He would be doing something, saying something, visiting with someone. But this time it was as if I was actually him.

I was lying in a bed. It was as if I was him, only not now. It was him before he passed. I was laying on a bed looking around a room. My vision was blurred but I could see several men walking around at the foot of my bed. My breathing was very shallow. I felt almost as if I was on a ventilator. After I thought about it, my guess was that it had to have been oxygen. I had sensed he was being drugged up and the blurred vision confirmed it. It was almost as if I had Vaseline smeared over my eyes.

Randy Phillips, from AEG, his contracting company, was going through a briefcase that seemed to be sitting on a dresser across from the foot of the bed. There were two others I couldn't see very clearly, but they too were looking through papers, with one that seemed to go in and out of the room.

My first impressions were that it was the day Michael died. He said he couldn't see and now I knew why. His vision was blurred, tremendously. I took to the autopsy reports. The one that concluded that Michael's death was considered a "homicide". There were boxes to check for the cause of death; Natural, Accident, Suicide, Could not be determined, and Homicide. If Dr. Conrad Murray "accidentally", as in manslaughter, killed Michael Jackson, I thought it should be noted. But it wasn't. The box checked was "Homicide" - Intraveneous injection by another, which fell in line with Michael saying "someone gave me a shot."

Further the indication of anatomic findings ascribed the death to: Acute Propofol Intoxication. Acute, meaning experienced to a severe or intense degree. Even a 'negligent' doctor wouldn't have rendered a determination for severe intoxication. This was purposeful and deliberate.

I looked into the drugs on the toxicology report that were found in Michael's system. Several of them could have caused the blurred vision; Lorazepam, Diazepam, Diethylpropion, and Lidocaine. All found in Michael's system per the toxicology report, are known to cause blurred vision. The autopsy was helpful, but it still didn't give me the whole picture.

Two days later, precisely, another vision came. I was a witness to it. It wasn't as if I was him, it was if I was watching from the background.

Michael had told me Frank Dileo was in the house the night he passed. Frank also had apologized for his part, but I never expected to see him in the room.

In the vision, Frank was sitting in a chair on the right side of Michael's bed. He was yelling at Michael that he screwed everything up. He said something to the effect of the hospital, the kids, the house, everything is gone now. Michael was crying.

It was unnerving. I was shocked when I then saw Frank insert a needle into a vial at Michael's right leg.

It would be Michaels right if he was laying in the bed. I assumed it must have been an IV of some sort. Frank then sat in the chair to the right of Michael again.

Randy Phillips was there again. He was going through a brown bag to the left of Michael, several feet from the foot of the bed. There must have been some kind of dresser there that the bag was on.

I'd like to say brief case but it was bigger. It seemed they were looking and taking things from his home.

When I awoke I could still hear Frank's voice in my head. It seemed like a Bronx accent. Like he could have been in a mafia movie.

It was apparent to me that they were canceling the shows and blaming Michael for it.

Later an email discovered in the AEG vs Katherine Jackson file confirmed it for me. On March 25, 2009, an email was sent by Randy Phillips of AEG to Paul Gongaware of AEG stating "We need to pull the plug now. I will explain." And the statements made by Conrad Murray in his interview with police noted the same. Michael would have to cancel the shows.

Yet, the fact that Frank DiLeo inserted a needle into a vial, didn't make sense to me. I again, went to the autopsy report and evidence collected from the trials.

In review of the findings, I noted that there was an IV placed an Michael's right leg. The vial I saw was what the medication would have been injected into. That held true, as well as the chair. Photos of Michael's home and his bedroom showed his bed with the chair I saw at the right side of his bed.

Further testimony by Jamie Lintemoot, the LA Coroner Toxicologist, revealed there was Propofol and Lidocaine found in the syringe found at Michael's bedside. She also noted the evidence of Propofol and Lidocaine in the syringe and short tubing found in the IV, which would indicate the injection into the IV by Frank DiLeo.

So now I had confirmations of two injections. One by Conrad Murray, another by Frank DiLeo, but still no injection that seemed to indicate a "shot" as Michael had described to me, except for the evidence itself; the syringe found lying bedside with Propofol and Lidocaine in it.

The three men present in his room were Frank DiLeo, Randy Phillips and a third that still seemed blurry. I hoped that in the next few days more would come.

The autopsy results revealed that the levels of Propofol found in Michael's system were much higher at the time of his death, then when they tested. Repeated resuscitation attempts as well as testing diluted the Propofol, yet the hospital blood that tested at was at 4.1. It was enough for a patient under general anesthesia and for that patient not to have control over their normal reflexes and breathing. This also supported several injections to me. By more than just Dr. Murray himself.

Michael had fired Frank DiLeo years before. I found it odd that he would be back in his life, so I started to do some research.

Apparently Tohme Tohme, Michael's manager at the beginning of the "This is It" shows, was fired by Michael that March. Tohme was auctioning off Michael's belongings at Neverland. Michael fired him later that month. In June, emails from Randy Phillips explained there was "no lawyer in place or a real manager." He claimed he called Frank DiLeo and John Branca in, just weeks before Michael passed. Both men Michael distrusted and had fired in the past and both sat on the board for Sony. DiLeo being appointed to the board after Michael's death.

Michael had me do a blog post at one time. It was early in the trial for Conrad Murray. He said simply that he hadn't hired a new manager yet. I didn't think much of it at the time, but now as I looked back I saw the importance of the information. He didn't hire DiLeo, Randy Phllips did.

In the coming months and after Michael's death, court records show payments being made to Frank DiLeo from AEG Live directly. Payments they seemed to be hiding from even the Estate of Michael Jackson.

I found it even more disturbing when Michael Amir Williams testified at the Conrad Murray trial stating that after Michael was pronounced dead at the hospital, Frank DiLeo blurted out "Your daddy had a heart attack and died." Michael Amir said he corrected him, saying not to say that. "They didn't know what happened."

But it was the fact that Frank said he phoned Randy Phillips and both said Michael was ill, Michael was having trouble breathing, both with no way of knowing. Not only that, but in the months prior to signing Michael on, there were emails exchanged by Randy Phillips and Tohme Tohme about Michael's apparent drug use.

On December 7, 2008, even before the contract was signed, an email was sent forwarding an article relating to Michael suffering in productivity from alleged alcohol and prescription medication. The article cited was a piece done by Diane Diamond.

A google search lead me to a case just prior to that signing. In 2008, a homicide from Propofol occurred in Alabama, when a man named Billy Shaw died from what was initially believed to be a heart attack. A year later, however, after his body was exhumed, toxicology results revealed a high concentration of Propofol – enough to kill him -- in his blood stream at the time of his death.

Prosecutors contended that 32-year-old Karri Denise Willoughby, Shaw's stepdaughter, had siphoned money from the bank accounts of her stepfather. She stole her mother's identity for financial gain. When the theft was discovered, Willoughby's access to the accounts was cut off. Being cut off from the money, prosecutors say, was Willoughby's motive for killing Shaw. Willoughby, who was a registered nurse, was arrested and charged with capital murder.

It sounded eerily similar. If you remember the initial autopsy report for Michael Jackson it also stated "heart attack". After the second autopsy was done, the new findings were 'Homicide – injection by another."

THE FINAL VISION

It wasn't until 2014 that I received the vision I had been waiting for. I tried to conceive of every possibility; a strange assistant to Conrad Murray, delivering the final dose. Perhaps even I was wrong, and it was Frank DiLeo or Conrad Murray himself. But as I laid in shavasana that evening in yoga, Michael approached. "Are you ready?", he said. In my mind I was thinking "Ready for what?". "Sure. I'm ready." I said, not knowing what he was talking about.

Maybe I had thought we were going to go on a trip, he'd show me scenes from the afterlife, but as the picture unfolded, I found myself in his bedroom again. Michael was laying on the bed and as I seemed to be watching from the foot of his bed, I saw a man approach him.

As he told me before, his hair was brown, he had a white short sleeved shirt on and I suddenly realized it was Michael's manager or former manager – Tohme Tohme.

He approached Michael's bedside on the same side Frank had been sitting at. No one else was in the room at the time. As I watched he tied a rubber hose around Michael's right arm and inserted a needle. This was it. The final shot that killed him, instantly as he said, and I opened my eyes in devastation.

In the next days I tried to get my head wrapped around the idea. Of all the scenarios I tried to come up with, this was definitely not one of them. Why would Tohme Tohme, Michael's own manager at one time, want to kill him?

I decided to begin to look for evidence of intent. If it was true, there must be some kind of evidence to support it. I had NO IDEA how much there actually was.

Tohme had been a broker. He started his business with Michael at the finding of financing for Neverland. That financing was with Colony Capital, one of Tohme's partners, as one email explained. In return for financing Neverland, Michael would be expected to perform a series of concerts with another friend of Colony Capital, Phillip Anshultz of AEG Live.

The financing of Neverland was backed with the same security as the backing for the series of the "This is It" concert series – Michael's Sony/ATV catalog. Once Michael engaged Tohme for his services, Tohme gained control over all of Michael's financial affairs, even negotiating with Sony themselves for royalties, which Tohme collected himself, from Michael's catalogs.

The contract Michael entered into with AEG was agreed upon by Tohme and Randy Phillips of AEG. Citing the catalog, once again, should the concerts not go on. Phillips showed early on he didn't think Michael was prepared. Yet both him and Tohme continued to add concert dates on to the tour. Selling tickets to the shows entitled Tohme to not only his salary of $100,000 per month from AEG but also a percentage from Michael and his contract.

The $100,000 per month Tohme would receive were said to be under a "separate" contract being payable to TT

International. He even had wire transfers to his own account based on the money Michael was supposed to receive from the concerts. Of course all of this was secured by additional collateral – the Sony/ATV catalog of songs Michael spoke about.

Tohme boasted he found Michael a home in LA on a street called Carolwood. A home he maintained control of and its staff. Hours after Michael had passed, he fired all of them. Locking the home up.

But Michael had fired Tohme after finding out he was auctioning off all of his belonging from his Neverland home earlier that year, so why was Tohme still around at the time of Michael's death?

It became apparent when the Estate for Michael Jackson began litigation with Tohme Tohme. The Estate claimed Tohme was taking advantage of Michael financially, and claims were made that the attorneys for the estate had enough evidence to put Tohme away for a very long time. He had been signing Michael's name and acting as a representative for Michael's company without any fiduciary right.

Other evidence became apparent as well. The testimony of Prince and Paris Jackson came to my attention again and finally I had put it all in perspective. Prince testified at the AEG vs Jackson trial that Michael would often cry after conversations with Randy Phillips, stating he thought they were out to kill him, referring to Tohme Tohme and Randy Phillips. He would say, 'They're going to kill me, they're going to kill me.'

A spiritual advisor for Michael, named June Gatlin had done an interview that played Michael's voice. In it he stated there was a divide between him and his representatives. He said he didn't talk to his lawyers or his accountants. He talked to Tohme and he talked to them. He had no idea what was in his accounts.

Other news footage shown, such as scenes from Geraldo at Large, stated Tohme said he would bring "death and destruction to the Jackson family".

The final account came while I reviewed the documents on file. It was the insurance policy. The one that Frank DiLeo mentioned, Elizabeth Taylor told me about, the one that Chernoff, Conrad Murray's attorney tried to bring up in the trial. The insurance policy purchased by AEG had a special "amendment". One that included a death clause that named an additional insured: Tohme Tohme. It also had an insured company called "The Mark Jones Company, LLC" which the policy underwriters deemed as a "fictitious" company.

They also contended that AEG and/or Jackson LLC had purported to assign their rights under the policy to the Estate of Michael Jackson, and that AEG and/or Jackson LLC never sought nor requested underwriters prior written consent to a purported assignment of their rights under the policy to the Estate.

The Estate of Michael Jackson claimed Michael's death was an "accident" under the policy. Under California Law, a policy that insures against "accidental death" requires only that the insured's death was not designed or anticipated by the insured. An accidental death is an unintended and undesignated result even if caused by the insured's voluntary act. But this was not an unintended event, nor was it caused by Michael's voluntary actions. His death was listed as "Homicide" and purposefully done by the hand of Tohme Tohme.

Even though AEG had dropped its claim on the insurance when emails from the company and their treatment of Michael surfaced, the Michael Jackson Estate did not. That case was settled in January, 2014 under "confidential terms".

The insurance was a major factor in this case. In the filing under "Table of Content: item II. Statement of Disputed Material facts Item F reads "underwriters agree to Issue Accident, But not Illness Coverage" Accident coverage was the only coverage in effect at the time of Michael Jacksons death. When in fact shows were to begin on 7/7/2009 there was no cancellation insurance. "Accident" coverage in this case was in fact "accidental death" insurance.

It was on 6/24/2009, the night before Michael's death, that the underwriters insisted on an in depth medical exam before agreeing to cover "illness." Michael had passed an examination that January and was found to be in good health. Now, however, we know by the emails discovered from AEG, that Michael was not in any shape to pass another physical examination.

Having been fired from Michael, Tohme was no longer entitled to his cut from the deals he brokered for Michael. AEG was at that time having trouble with the insurance. That was evidenced from Conrad Murray's emails to the insurance company not even an hour before Michael's death. How would AEG and Tohme recoup their costs and fees if they didn't have insurance?

The tour agreement said that the Michael Jackson Co was ultimately liable to pay all tour costs in the event they were not recouped from the shows. If the tour was cancelled and the re-coup from Michael could not be covered, insurance would need to be used to help offset the costs.

Costs Randy Phillips himself stated were in the millions and that he was so concerned about.

But Michael couldn't pass the physical necessary for cancellation insurance. It was Conrad Murray himself that spoke of the cancellation of the shows in his statement to the LAPD. The insurance policy was initialed into effect on June 22, 2009 naming Tohme as additional insured upon accidental death, three days before Michael passed. Meanwhile the insurers were still trying to get the requested information from the doctor for "illness" coverage.

Michael was too weak to perform. Tohme was brokering a deal with Sony for his catalogs, even collecting on the royalties from them and making sure he received a salary from AEG. If he thought Michael would be able to perform, why wouldn't he just wait and get the percentage Michael would have gotten from the shows?

Instead he was taking a salary directly from AEG as well. Without funds from the insurance they would only receive the catalog in the hands of AEG, but that same catalog was used in other places with other creditors.

The people who were after that famed catalog all along and the attorney that showed back up in Michael's life by the request of Randy Phillips days before he passed: John Branca would get what he wanted after all. John Branca and Frank DiLeo were both shareholders for Sony. And the man brokering all the deals and at the center of it all was Tohme Tohme.

Sony was in the red at this time. Since 2008 Sony corporation had been reporting losses. In April, 2012 it was announced Sony was cutting 10,000 jobs worldwide after four years in the red. Sony themselves announced in

December, 2008 cuts of 16,000 workers after the global financial crisis. In 2012 the company expected \$2.7 billion in net losses.

Conrad Murray was giving Michael medications for the three months leading to his death. In an email dated May 28, 2009, discovered in the AEG vs Katherine Jackson trial, Murray said he was performing and was continuing to fulfill his services to the "client" in good faith. He was asking for his monthly fee that was still not being paid.

Although an email from Paul Gongaware of AEG to Michael Amir Williams on 5/6/2009 stated his term of service was a "done deal". Murray would be paid \$150,000 per month, he only needed ten days to wind down his practice then he would be "full time".

Other emails from Paul Gongaware of AEG in June, 2009 stated that they were having a face to face with the Dr. He needed to be reminded that it was AEG, not MJ, that was paying his salary and they wanted him to understand what was expected of him.

Later AEG submitted Murray's salary of \$300,000 to the Estate of Michael Jackson listed under production costs for reimbursement.

Phone records during the trials showed a phone call from Dr. Murray to Randy Phillips of AEG that Phillips said lasted three minutes. The phone call was on record for twenty five minutes and was just prior to the "meeting" with the Dr.

Murray was giving Michael diet pills. A substance called Ephedrine which causes rapid weight loss. Karen Faye, Michael's makeup artist testified Michael lost about 15 pounds in the week before he passed. Michael was unable to perform, while Murray ordered large amounts of Propofol and administered other drugs taxing his system. It was during the trial that a doctor had even advised that Michael should be brought to the hospital right away after he learned of his symptoms. The doctor said they were classic symptoms of poisoning.

But I don't think Dr. Murray had any idea why AEG was stalling to sign his contract and not paying him. I don't think they ever intended on Murray actually being paid even though the contract agreement cited his services to begin on May 1, 2009. A contract that required Dr. Murray to even have a qualified medical assistant "approved" by the Producer, AEG. He was required to "perform the services reasonably requested by Producer" and also name the Producer (AEG) and its affiliates as additional insureds on insurance policies he was to hold.

As with all notices of contractual obligations, the agreement named the parties to be delivered to by US postal mail; AEG Live Productions LLC, GCA Holdings LLC (Murray's company) and Michael Jackson. All addresses were listed appropriately, with the exception of Michael Jackson himself.

In an email dated 5/8/2009, Timm Woolley from AEG emailed Dr Murray letting him know that the AEG contract would not cover more than one month in lieu of notice if there was a curtailment or cessation of the tour. He also cited loss of profit and other insurances, such as accident, that could cover him in case he was "prevented" from providing his services. It seemed very generous to be looking out for Murray, considering AEG contended Murray was "Michael's" personal physician and only an independent contractor to be paid through AEG.

Randy Phillips even wrote an email on August 18, 2009, stating that he thought he knew what killed MJ and thought it would exonerate Dr. Murray.

However, prior to that email, we find that AEG themselves indicated that their expectations for the tour to be fulfilled would not happen. Emails dated April 24, 2009 between AEG executives Timm Woolley, Paul Gongaware and Shawn Trell discussed "break even" insurance, citing examples that if they were not able to get past show 6 that they would be able to "recoup" three shows. They cited "Dr. T's" separation, rescheduled shows, and "Daily Mail" articles that could cause a withdrawal of the $8 million behind the $17.5 million coverage that would lead to a collapse of the "deal". Coverage needed to be secured as soon as possible.

LOOKING BACK

When I looked back at the announcement of Michael's death at UCLA hospital, I finally realized it was Tohme Tohme there standing with Jermaine Jackson, as once described by Michael; His dark brown hair, white short sleeved shirt, and an open collar. Jermaine, he said, would be the only spokesperson for the family.

It was on 1/26/09 that Tohme even forwarded an email about Michael's apparent drug use to AEG executive Randy Phillips. Just as the concert preparations were to begin. It was that same day that Phillips forwarded the contract for Michael to Tohme Tohme to do the concerts.

Signatures on that contract, one from the Michael Jackson Co. and the other from Michael Jackson himself, read Michael Jackson. But both signatures were vastly different.

The contract stated that in all cases the Artisco (Michael's company that Tohme was controlling) would receive payment. In all cases it was Tohme and Phillips that had to agree that Michael actually performed, before any payment would be made to the "Artist". When payment was agreed upon, even that payment would be less costs for production, even less insurance premiums for AEG and Tohme's salary, and then wire transferred to the "Artistco", aka Tohme Tohme.

The mere fact that they had to agree he actually performed told me even from the beginning an impersonator must have been on stand-by.

According to the contract Tohme's 15% would be added to pool expenses, as well as his salary of $100,000 a month, not to mention the separate contract he had with Michael for $35,000 a month. Those pool expenses would again be subtracted from "Artist".

Cancellation insurance was written to the effect to not only cover "pool expenses" that Michael was already being held responsible for, but for profits as well. Additionally, $100,000 per month for rent on the home on Carolwood was to be subtracted as well. A home that was secured by Tohme Tohme himself.

Five million dollars was also advanced to Tohme with $3,000,000 going to Two Seas Records and $2,000,000 going directly to Tohme again.

Rolling Stones Magazine wrote that March that Dr Tohme Tohme and Randy Phillips, the CEO of AEG said the pop stars stake in Sony/ATV Music Publishing, which owns the Beatles catalog, was keeping Jackson afloat, but he had borrowed hundreds of millions of dollars against that investment.

Tohme was formally terminated by Michael by written notice on May 5, 2009, yet AEG kept Tohme around. Even to the point of having him sign on behalf of the Michael Jackson Co., with full knowledge that Tohme was not authorized to represent Michael or his company any longer after Michael's death. His signing on behalf of the company entitled them both to sell the video footage taken from Michael's rehearsals to the Estate that Sunday, and in turn, make another tidy profit.

I guess that's why Phillips was so excited about his deal on July 2, boasting about how much money they would make in his emails and to the press.

Tohme had told Phillips of AEG that Michael was in dire financial straits; in other words he would be an easy in. He made sure he stated numerous times, that Jermaine was the only one who was authorized to speak on behalf of the family at the announcement of Michael's death and to the New York Times, when attorney Brian Oxman spoke out that Michael had been surrounded by "disreputable people".

Further inquiry revealed photos taken of both Tohme and Phillips arriving at UCLA together the day Michael was pronounced dead. Phillips was quoted in the Los Angeles Times in late May, 2009, as saying the O2 shows were a "do or die" moment for MJ.

When a reporter wrote in March of 2009 that Randy Phillips had the satisfied look of a man who had just pulled off an inconceivably ambitious plan, I don't think she realized just how inconceivable that plan was.

ALL ROADS LEAD TO SONY

It was later discovered in court testimony that there was also a belief that Al Malnik, Tommy Matolla and John Branca had offshore accounts; all with deposits from Sony. I guess that's why Michael might have said Sony=Mattola.

Fox News published an article on July 12, 2002 that told of a standoff between Tommy Mottola and Michael Jackson. The source said that on more than one occasion he was present while Sony Music President Tommy Mottola threatened Jackson. Saying his career would be destroyed if he didn't agree to Tommy's terms. The source said it was an effort to squeeze Michael financially and simply put, Tommy wanted the Beatles catalog.

Copyrights for Michael's catalog were transferred on May 29, 2009 and recorded on June 4, 2009, just weeks before Michael's death. Michael's loans on the catalog were transferred from Bank of America to WMG Acquisition Corporation and Party 2: Wells Fargo:

Document Number: V3579D650
Date of Recordation: 2009-06-04
Entire Copyright Document: V3579 D640-676 P1-802

WMG Acquisition Corp., is Warner Music and operates as a music content company in United States and internationally. It engages in recorded music and music publishing. It does marketing, distribution, and licensing of recorded music in various physical and digital formats. It also does artist management, merchandising, strategic marketing and brand management, ticketing, concert promotion, fan club, original programming, and video entertainment.

As for the famed catalog that Michael owned half of, it was under the name of Sony/ATV. His 50 percent share in the Sony-ATV Music Publishing catalog, was valued between $1.5 billion and $2 billion in 2009. The partnership itself was about $600 million in debt in 2009 and is recognized as the shrewdest business move of Michael's career. He bought the catalog containing hits from the Beatles in 1985 for $47.5 million. In the early 2000s, he borrowed $300 million against the catalog. That made the value of Michael's share in 2009, less debt, worth between $150 million and $400 million. Hardly someone whom the press and others would claim as broke. Controlled maybe, but certainly not broke.

In summary, the findings on the autopsy report for Michael Jackson were "Homicide". For the levels of Propofol in his system to conclude these findings it would stand to reason that there was more than one injection of the substance given. Three injections, as we've stated here, however, would indicate the amounts in line with the autopsy findings.

For further confirmations on the evidence and information provided in this book please review the corresponding documents. The autopsy reports support the injection sites as noted in this book. The inner arm and leg both contain puncture wounds. The levels of Propofol are noted on the toxicology report as well as the other drugs that would induce "blurred vision".

Additional findings are in the copy of the contract with AEG and insurance policy noting Tohme Tohme as additional insured that can be found in the court documents on file with the State of California in the AEG vs Katherine Jackson case as well as the Lloyds of London vs AEG case (Case No BC462973).

In 2003 Michael Jackson formally terminated his relationship with John Branca and demanded the return of the will he is currently using to run the Michael Jackson Estate. The will in question was noted as being signed by Michael in Los Angeles on July 7, 2002. Al Sharpton has refuted this claim. He has produced video footage of Michael Jackson alongside of him in New York City that day. The Estate contends the will was signed by Michael in Los Angeles on the same date.

The will was drafted in 1997, but Branca says it wasn't done by him. Instead, he said he assigned it to a member of his firm who specialized in wills and trusts. It was redone in 2002, after the birth of Michael's third child. It is probable that since the will was drafted by Branca's firm, it was retained as well.

John Branca was a subject of investigation for conspiracy and embezzlement during Michael's 2005 child molestation charge and during a private investigation, it was discovered that there was an "improper" relationship between Branca and Tommy Mottola. Both men were allegedly funneling Michael's money to offshore accounts in the Caribbean. (Interfor report, April 15, 2003)

The will in question is an ongoing issue. As of 1/1/2014, the probate estate was still pending for John Branca and John McClain at the Superior Court of California, County of Los Angeles, Case No BP 117321.

It is rumored that in February/March of 2009 Michael told both Tohme and attorney Dennis Hawk that he had no will and needed one. Hawk is said to be a friend of former Estate executor Barry Seigel, who resigned his position from being an executor of the Estate on August 26, 2003.

On March 25, 2009 one of Michael's associates, Jeff Cannon, was let go. Someone who identified themselves as Michael's assistant (a title given to Michael Amir Williams of security) phoned Jeff with the news. Barry Siegel was then again back in the picture. In the letter of termination for Mr. Cannon, all records, books and other documents were requested to be sent to Barry Siegel at Provident Financial Management in Santa Monica, CA.

It was Michael who also told me, as I stated in my previous book, **Another Part of Me**, that he was redoing his will later that May. An attorney named Sean Najerian was working on the details. I was divorcing at the time and Michael thought it best that I have a house. At the time I didn't think too much of it. Only that he was getting his affairs in order. Now as I look back, I see how serious the matter actually was.

Michael's attorney, Peter Lopez, was also apparently let go of in April that year for unknown reasons. Leaving Michael in the hands of the AEG attorney, Joel Katz, another Sony boardmember.

In July, 2009 it was reported that the Estate of Michael Jackson refused to allow Katherine Jackson, Michael's mother, the ability to view the contract between her son and AEG. There was also a filing at that time by AEG lawyers against Katherine because she and her attorneys refused to sign a confidentiality agreement. That agreement would have barred her from using the information contained in the AEG contract in any legal process other than in probate court.

Currently there is another opportunity for appeal with the Katherine Jackson and AEG case through counsel in January, 2015. (Case No BC445597 Superior Court of the State of California, County of Los Angeles)

During the last trial Randy Phillips of AEG was impeached 43 times. For instance when Randy was asked if Kenny Ortega was complaining about Michael's health he outright said "no".

Conrad Murray has been trying repeatedly to get an appeal asking for testing of the residue of a 100 ml bottle of Propofol that prosecutors say contained the fatal dose of the surgical anesthetic and requesting fingerprint testing for the "two syringes" and the IV bag found at the home. He continues to contend that he only injected a small dose the morning Michael died.

Propofol expert, Dr. Paul White, testified at the Conrad Murray trial. When he was asked if that the doctors care could result in death, White said if the Propofol IV "came opened up widely", significant amounts at one time, you could achieve a significant effect that could result in cardiopulmonary arrest, as was stated on the autopsy. White stated that he didn't believe that Murray's dose of Propofol caused Michael's death.

Even the levels of Lidocaine found during the autopsy should have been "0". Lidocaine, he said, has a half-life and as hours progress, so does the levels found in the body. Lidocaine was still present in Michael Jacksons blood at the time of autopsy. The blood specimens taken were on the date of his death, June 25, 2009, at 1:30 pm. For Lidocaine to still to be present, injection, most likely with the Propofol, must have been given that day late morning. The time frame that Randy Phillips had noted when he first responded to questioning in the Conrad Murray trial.

Propofol has a half-life of 2-24 hours. Based on the levels of Propofol found in Michael's urine samples, another testimony from a Dr. Steven Shafer, noted that Michael must have been given **more than** 2000 mg of Propofol in order for the urine specimens to fall in line with the toxicology findings. Two thousand milligrams may be typically associated with those undergoing major surgery for a period of approximately 2 ½ hours.

Conrad Murray was found guilty of "involuntary manslaughter" on November 7, 2011. The case, however, was categorized as a "criminal homicide" by LAPD, not medical malpractice.

The Estate of Michael Jackson filed a complaint on Tohme Tohme on 2/17/12 (Case No BP117321 Superior Court for the State of California, County of Los Angeles) They contended that Tohme took control of all of Michael's personal and professional affairs. That with no oversight he installed a very lucrative financial package for himself obtained as a result of a manifest breach of his fiduciary duties. Tohme used his powers as Michael's fiduciary and agent to take possession of both money and valuable personal property belonging to Michael that he never returned to Michael or the Executors.

Tohme also filed a counter complaint against the Estate (Case No SC115988) on 6/6/12, contending that there are fictitious defendants in the Estates suit against him and they are subject to legal liability. Eerily similar to the allegations made by Lloyds Insurance regarding "The Mark

Jones Co." named on the AEG insurance policy.

Tohme contends that he was Michael's "only" manager, which still leaves the question of how or why Frank DiLeo was back in the picture.

An agreement for DiLeo and Michael was produced at trial, dated 6/5/2009, but that agreement was never signed.

Tohme also stated:

- That he arranged for the leasing of the rental home that Michael died in. (which would make one think he might have access to that home.)
- He provided footage for the making of the "This is It" movie. (Apparently, this must have been alongside AEG since they were the ones that filed copyrights for it.)
- He is owed 2.3 million dollars for a finders fee for obtaining financing for Neverland Ranch.
- Was keeping money to purchase a permanent home of which Michael had dreamed.
- Suggested "This is It" for the title of the shows.
- *Since August, 2008 he was the representative for Michael for SONY/ATV and worked with advisors regarding auditing and refinancing contracts with Sony/ATV.*
- Tohme said he managed scheduling arrangements with **AEG** representatives and oversaw transportation and **SECURITY.**
- Accepted Michael's royalty payments from Sony (so Michael could buy a home) ** Actually this was part of Michael's contract with AEG. The funds were to be advanced as a line of credit to buy his home in Vegas. Albeit advanced to Tohme.**

- Voluntarily handed over the 5.5 million dollars to the Estate that he was holding for Michael.
- He cited his services agreement dated 7/2/2008 where he began to negotiate and manage housing and personal business matters for Michael.
- *Coordinated with SONY*
- Assisted in live and *TAPED performances*.
- *Provided the material for the feature film "This is It"*

Please keep in mind Tohme was wire transferring an additional $35,000 a month for his services. He also, according to this filing, wanted his 15% of all the earnings Michael had from 8/2008 to date. He stated that Michael and the Estate had breached the services agreement by failing to pay the compensation due.

I think if Michael had just the royalty payments from the catalog, the 5.5 million dollars, he could have moved on with his life without Tohme or AEG. They, together, made it impossible for him to leave the situation without walking away from literally everything he owned.

Dr. Tohme Tohme has been reported as having no medical license in any state in the US and has a litany of fraudulent real estate loans.

On January 22, 2009, AEG counsel Kathy Jorrie sent an email requesting a background check on Tohme, stating someone at AEG should meet with Michael to make sure he understood what he was entering into. To date I have not found evidence indicating that was ever done.

After Michael's death Tohme stated that AEG had to get insurance and Michael had a 4 hour physical by a doctor chosen by the insurance company. He said for a guy to go on and dance for 4 hours, not even an athlete could do that, and Michael was doing it at rehearsal every day. I guess we all know better now.

As evidenced in the Estate of Michael Jackson's lawsuit filed on 2/17/2012, Tohme Tohme was terminated by Michael in March, 2009. Emails discovered from the AEG vs Katherine Jackson suit dated 4/24/09 reference Tohme's separation from Michael.

Regardless, the insurance policy AEG put into place that was enforced on June 22, 2009, three days before Michael was pronounced dead, still had Tohme Tohme's name added to an amendment of the policy and was named as "additional insured" covered under "accidental death."

Michael Jackson announced the "This is It" series of shows on March 5, 2009. Three months later he was pronounced dead. We owe it to his legacy to speak the truth on his behalf and have him be remembered for the entertainer and humanitarian he was amidst the lies and manipulation the industry and press have so undeservingly thrown on him.

THE AUTOPSY REPORT FINDINGS

The first autopsy was conducted on 6/26/2009
Case No 2009-04415

Synopsis: The decedent is a 50 year old black male who suffered respiratory arrest while at home under the care of his primary physician. (Heart Attack)

Accident/Natural

FINAL autopsy and medical evidence analysis report was done 8/07/09, as requested by the family.

Manner of death: Homicide – Acute (present or experienced to a severe or intense degree) Propofol Intoxication

The anatomical summary findings revealed propofol, lorazepam, midazolam, lidocaine, diazepam and nordiazepam, identified in blood samples.

Propofol, midazolam, lidocaine and ephedrine (diet pills) identified in the urine.

Propofol and lidocaine identified in liver tissue.

Propofol identified in the vitreous humor and lidocaine and propofol were identified in the stomach contents.

- Propofol is used to sedate patients for surgery. Known as "going under"
- Lorazepam is a sedative/muscle relaxer
- Midazolam is a sedative to treat insomnia
- Lidocaine is a local anesthetic typically used topically to relieve itching, burning, and pain from skin inflammations. It's also injected as a dental anesthetic, or used as a local anesthetic for minor surgery.
- Diazepam is used to treat insomnia, anxiety and benzodiazepine withdrawl. Benzo withdrawl is due to taking medication as prescribed - someone suffering from withdrawal is not necessarily a "drug addict." Benzo withdrawal is characterized by severe sleep disturbances, irritability, increased tension and anxiety, panic attacks, hand tremors, sweating, difficulty with concentration, confusion and cognitive difficulty, memory problems, dry retching and nausea, weight loss, palpitations, headache, muscular pain and stiffness. All traits noted by team members at the rehearsals for the "This is It" concerts.
- Nordiazepam is used to treat anxiety
- Ephedrine is a stimulant and appetite suppressant

The opinion rendered the manner of death a homicide due to the toxicological findings of high blood concentrations of propofol as well as the presence of benzodiazepines.

The circumstances indicated that propofol and the benzodiazepines were administered by another and the circumstance *did not support self-administration* of propofol.

The propofol was administered in a non-hospital setting without any appropriate medical indication.

There were punctures and contusions of the right neck, both arms, the left calf and right ankle which coincided with the visions received. One on Michael's inner right arm and the puncture mark that would have been from the IV at his ankle I saw.

Puncture marks were also noted at the right shoulder on the diagram. This fell in line with Michael's statement to me early on.

The levels of propofol were found on the summary of toxicological findings. Heart blood was at 3.2 ml, hospital blood at 4.1 ml, femoral blood 2.6 ml, liver 6.2 ml. gastric contents .13 ml, urine .15 ml.

The levels of the other benzodiazepines (Lidocaine, Diazepam, Nordiazepam, Lorazepam and Midazolam) were significantly less. Ephedrine was found present in the urine specimen.

The Los Angeles County Coroner's finding was that there was no Demerol or any other opiates in Michael Jacksons body at the time of his death. They did not find any of the signs typically associated with a **_drug "addict"_** on his body.

MEDICAL EVIDENCE COLLECTED AT THE SCENE

- Propofol and Lidocaine were detected in approximately .19 g of white fluid from a 10cc syringe barrel with plunger.
- Four components of the IV system were tested.
  - Propofol, Lidocaine and Flumazenil were detected in approximately .17g of white tinted fluid from a 10cc syringe.
  - Propofol, Lidocaine, and Flumazenil were detected in approximately .47g of yellow tinted fluid from a short section of IV tubing attached to a Y connector.
  - No drugs were detected in approximately 17g of clear liquid from a long section of IV tubing attached to an IV bag plug.
  - No drugs were detected in approximately .38g of clear fluid from a 1000cc IV bag.

**Note: Flumazenil reverses the effects of sedation. Flumazenil is administered intravenously to counteract the effects of benzodiazepines including sedation and memory loss.

***Special Note: These items were not tested for fingerprints. Conrad Murray and his legal team have been trying to get a court appeal for the last few years asking for the testing of these items.   To date they have been unsuccessful.

Again the findings correspond with the visions.   Both apparatuses used are present.   A plunger used for the "shot" in the arm area and an IV system found at the leg used for the other injections. The items being left behind on the scene indicates either Conrad Murray didn't clean everything up he intended to, or these items were not used by him.

ABOUT THE AUTHOR

Deborah Stefaniak is a psychic, medium and author. Her psychic connection to Michael Jackson has been documented in her book *Another Part of Me – An Extraordinary Tale of Twin Souls*. Twin souls are part of the same soul, like two physical twins created from the same cells. They share a special bond and connection beyond the body.

For all general purposes, just think of it as she is just another psychic/medium able to connect with the other side.

Made in the USA
Lexington, KY
24 June 2017